William Morris
and
The Arts and Crafts Movement

A DESIGN SOURCE BOOK

by

Linda Parry
of the Victoria and Albert Museum, London

with an essay on
Textiles of the American Arts and Crafts Movement

by
Gillian Moss
of the Cooper-Hewitt Museum, New York

PORTLAND HOUSE
NEW YORK

Acknowledgements

Most of the Art and Crafts patterns illustrated in this book are taken from the collections of the Victoria and Albert Museum. I would like to thank my colleagues in the Department of Textiles and Dress, Mike Kitkatt and Daniel McGrath, who took most of the photographs, and Isobel Sinden and Edwin Wallace of the Picture Library for making this a comparatively painless exercise.

Selecting items from other collections has also been made easier with the help of a number of colleagues and friends; Ann Lynch and Audrey Duck of G.P. & J. Baker and Mark Turner of the Silver Studio Collection at Middlesex Polytechnic deserve special thanks. I would also like to thank: the Cooper-Hewitt Museum, New York; Rhode Island School of Design; Nordenfjeldske Kunstindustrimuseum, Trondheim; Kunstindustrimuseet Oslo; Museum of Decorative Arts, Copenhagen; Wurttembergisches Landesmuseum, Stuttgart; Deutsches Textilemuseum, Krefeld; Museum fur angewandte Kunst, Vienna. By listing only the collections of European and American museums I hope that the many individuals who have also assisted will also accept my sincere appreciation.

The process of putting the book together has been very pleasurable thanks both to Peggy Vance and Jane Rogoyska and I am delighted to have been part of this joint Anglo-American study.

Published by Portland House
a division of dilithium Press, Ltd.
Distributed by Crown Publishers, Inc.
225 Park Avenue South
New York New York 10003

William Morris and The Arts and Crafts Movement
contains a selection of designs and patterns from
The Victoria and Albert Museum
Cromwell Rd., London SW7

and

other Museums in Europe and the USA

ISBN 0–517–69260–0

Printed in Malaysia

h g f e d b a

Introduction

The first exhibition of the Arts and Crafts Exhibition Society in 1888 coincided with a period of revived interest in all aspects of British decorative design and manufacture whether completed in the home, the workshop or the factory. This change was brought about mostly due to the influence of one man: William Morris (1834–96). His ideas on pattern-making, manufacture and the philosophy of work inspired not only individual designers and craftsmen, but also those involved in large-scale commercial manufacture. The effects that this had in Britain, manifested in the formation of a new exhibiting society, provided a union of purpose in the arts not seen since the Middle Ages.

WILLIAM MORRIS

Despite Morris's early ambition to be a painter and his later reputation as writer, poet, publisher, political thinker and activist, it is as a designer of patterns that he is most widely known today. His designs provided a mirror for his soul, reflecting his greatest artistic interests and influences. In most of his work historical patterns combine together with British floral forms. Just as these show both his antiquarian interests and love of the British countryside, his colouring derived from traditional dyes and glazes and his choice of texture and form from the effects he most admired in the work of past craftsmen. Despite such eclecticism, his patterns show great originality; a successful union of ideas that many later designers adopted in their own work.

Morris's first commercial designs, for embroideries and wallpapers, were drawn in the 1860s, over twenty years before the first Arts and Crafts Exhibition. However, earlier narrative schemes, such as the Oxford Union murals (1857) and painted furniture made for his rooms at Red Lion Square in London (1856–9) show, through an abundance of decoration, an almost unconscious urge by the artist to draw patterns. Morris soon recognised this innate talent and spent the rest of his life designing and manufacturing those items he most wished to have around him.

Each of Morris's designs reflects his particular interests at the time it was drawn. His constantly inquiring mind moved from one manufacturing technique to another as each was understood and achieved. Early printed textiles (4b, 2a) show repeats influenced from designing wallpapers and tiles, whereas his embroideries change from patterns of repeating vertical and horizontal bands to single mirror-imaged compositions (11) as used in hand-knotted carpets. However, his earliest repeating designs do show, above all, his interest in nature.

NATURAL ORNAMENT

Flowers have proved the most popular subjects for all British textiles since the sixteenth century, and probably before. Morris, and the Arts and Crafts designers who followed, continued this trend but used these in an innovative, though typically British way. Morris chose unusual types of native hedgerow and garden plants. Many of these had been established in Britain for many centuries but had fallen out of favour and use. The increasing introduction of foreign plants into Britain, encouraged in the 1840s by the Royal Horticultural Society, triggered a fashion for hothouse palms and orchids and brightly coloured garden plants such as pelargoniums, fuchsias, rhododendrons and hydrangeas. These were enthusiastically adopted by the interior design trade and three-dimensional, densely grouped and brightly coloured designs soon became the stock in trade of every commercial manufacturer. Reacting against this, Morris chose such plants as marigolds (4b, 7), jasmine (5), crown imperial lilies (4a), honeysuckle (12b), and eyebright (16b), both in his own garden and for his patterns. Willow boughs and acanthus leaves provided both the background and structure for most of these (see 6a, 7, 10a, 12b, 9, 8a, 4a, 10b, 14b, 11, 16).

The natural colouring and growth patterns of each plant was of prime importance to Morris as these factors, above all, characterised the British countryside throughout the seasons. Flowers retain their natural forms in all his designs, and it is the pattern, not nature, that conforms. Colouring was equally important to the success of his patterns and with the use of plant dyes Morris was able to reproduce the natural effect he required, and to mix a number of different colours and shades within one design while still retaining a harmonious effect. This authority, gained from a deep knowledge and love of nature, also enabled him to include complex subsidiary designs in many of his patterns without confusing the main theme.

HISTORIC PATTERNS

The second greatest influence on Morris's career as a pattern-maker was, without doubt, his interest in historic design. Although this is not so evident in his early wallpapers and printed cottons, it proved of paramount importance in his later designs for carpets, woven textiles and embroideries. A knowledgeable art historian, Morris had, from the 1870s, been closely associated with the collections of the South Kensington Museum (now the Victoria and Albert Museum) both as visitor and advisor on acquisitions. Whether this concentrated study of Museum objects persuaded him to embark on commercial weaving (from 1876) or hand-knotted carpet manufacture (1878) is difficult to determine. What is certain is that from this period all his designs are more formal in structure, reflecting his dominating interest in Italian and Near Eastern ceramics and textiles. This provided a considerable change from the free-flowing Medieval-inspired patterns of the 1860s and 1870s.

Morris frequently lectured on the types of design he preferred and illustrated his lectures with examples of the most popular forms of traditional pattern. In describing his own work as constructed on either a "net" or "branch" framework, he categorised the basic structure of all repeating designs. The former, repeated in diamonds (or the traditional "ogee") provides a balanced effect, the latter an unsymmetrical meander. Morris's use of pattern forms was therefore not new, but his application of each was unusual. Whereas the use of symmetrical and unbalanced designs in the past has been determined by fashion, Morris used both contemporaneously. His main consideration in selecting which type of pattern he utilised was the technique for which each design was made. This is probably the single most important factor in his success as a designer: the appropriateness of the pattern for the purpose.

It was not simply inquisitiveness or a need for practical involvement that persuaded Morris to learn all the manufacturing methods adopted by Morris & Company. This technical knowledge made the process of designing easier, however intuitive and inventive his instincts.

MORRIS AND COMPANY

Having discussed Morris's methods of pattern-making in detail a little should also be said of his role as manufacturer. After all, however superficial it may seem, it is as a maker of wallpapers and textiles that he is best known today. He was responsible for setting up two manufacturing companies, the first, Morris, Marshall, Faulkner and Company in 1861 and, on its dissolution in 1875, Morris & Company, which continued to trade until 1940. Through these firms, Morris was responsible, at one time or another, for the manufacture of many forms of decorative art, including furniture, metalwork, glass, ceramics, wallpapers and textiles. Considering textile production alone, Morris & Company provided a comprehensive range of goods from hand-woven tapestries and carpets to embroideries, printed textiles, machine-woven carpets and no less than twenty different types of woven fabric. Although shops such as Liberty's of Regent Street were able to provide such a varied range, these were manufactured by a number of different firms. No other contemporary manufacturer offered such an unusual mixture of techniques nor did any other factory cope with such a prodigious workload.

Whereas Morris had the means and the knowledge to produce all of the goods he sold, some were manufactured for him by contractors. Following early unsuccessful experiments with block-printed wallpapers, Morris handed all further work to Jeffrey & Company, a London firm. The manager of the firm, Metford Warner, was a man of great insight and patience. It is some measure of his talents that Morris was content for Warner to supervise all of his wallpaper manufacture from this time, despite the use of artificial distemper colours, the unnatural effects of which he should not normally have liked. Of more limited success were early printed textiles produced by Thomas Wardle, a silk dyer at Leek in Staffordshire. Morris was able to take full control over the dyeing and printing of all new designs from 1881, when he moved to his own factory at Merton Abbey, near Wandsworth in Surrey.

Weaving, being a more specialised, time-consuming and exacting process, presented greater difficulties. It is likely that Morris, at one time or another, produced on the looms at Merton Abbey all the various types of woven fabric that he sold. However, with limited manpower and equipment some were produced for him by Northern firms. These included silk damasks in Macclesfield, gauzes, silk and wool double cloths in Darvel, Scotland, and heavy two- and three-ply woollen weaves in Yorkshire. Large orders were also woven by contractors.

The non-mechanised techniques of embroideries, hand-knotted carpets and tapestries provided Morris with his greatest personal achievements as a manufacturer. He continued to be involved with the design and supervision of embroidery work for twenty years but in 1885 appointed his youngest daughter,

May, as manager of this section of the firm. It is clear that his increasing preoccupation with carpet knotting and tapestry weaving left little time for the techniques, as from this time all new designs were drawn by May and Henry Dearle (17, 19). This concentration of interest on one technique at a time is one of the most interesting developments of Morris's career as a designer. In turn, with his increasing preoccupation with politics and book production in the late 1880s, his interest in textile production diminished. From this time, both the design and manufacture of Morris & Company's commercial textiles were left to others.

HENRY DEARLE AND LATER MORRIS PRODUCTION

It is likely that Morris retained his interest in Morris & Company until his death. it is known that he visited the Merton Abbey Works at least once a week in his later years and, at times, sat and drew patterns. However, it was his assistant, Henry Dearle (1860–1932), who took over supervision of most of the manufacturing side of the Works and, from 1888 (the year of the first Arts and Crafts exhibition), provided most of the repeating designs subsequently used.

Having been trained both as a designer and craftsman by Morris, Dearle's work is, at times, understandably derivative. However, by the 1890s, his work began to show increasing confidence and an original style emerged. This is exemplified in such patterns as Seaweed wallpaper (21a), Helena (20a) and Tulip (14a) which were woven textiles and Eden (12a), which was used for printed cotton. Dearle, as Manager of Merton Abbey and, on Morris's death, artistic director of Morris & Company, was far more directly involved in the Arts and Crafts Exhibitions than Morris himself. He was responsible for the many Morris exhibits which appeared at various shows and for supplying details of these for the catalogue. Ironically, this has been the main source of inaccurate information about the designs produced by Morris & Co. Most pieces were attributed to Morris as the founder of the company and as the most important and influential British designer. This greatly retarded recognition of Dearle's work for many years and it is only now that his career can be properly evaluated. May Morris's career can be said to have been similarly affected by her famous father. As an embroideress she had few peers; her work, whether using her own or others designs, was widely appreciated in artistic circles throughout her own lifetime and was widely exhibited, although it is through her teaching of the craft that most influence is felt today.

In an attempt to modernise their image and to improve sales in

[9]

the early years of the twentieth century Morris & Co. bought a few designs from free-lance designers. These included tapestry designs from some of the most fashionable artists and illustrators of the day and new ranges of wallpapers with designs by W.A.S. Benson and Katherine Kersey (18b) as well as Henry Dearle and May Morris. Such innovations were not wholly successful, however, and it was to other designers and manufacturers that the public turned to satisfy their need for new, original patterns and products.

The Arts and Crafts Exhibition Society

William Morris's versatility and originality as a designer of patterns have proved to be his most enduring monument, but it was through his views on society and manufacture that his influence on the Arts and Crafts Movement was felt the most. He believed that the importance placed on new technology in industry since the later eighteenth century had resulted in the gradual erosion of the role of the craftsman and the subsequent loss of traditional skills. The emphasis on speed and profits provided technically brilliant yet artistically dead products and the emphasis away from individual involvement and artistry had subsequently resulted in a marked decline in design. In his own workshops he provided attractive surroundings and interesting work as an incentive for his workmen to achieve the uncompromisingly good results which he demanded. Many adopted these views and, with a general improvement in art school training, it became essential that these new ideas and skills were seen, encouraged and practised.

The Arts and Crafts Exhibition Society was set up in 1887 by a number of leading designers, craftsmen and manufacturers, initially as a reaction against the Royal Academy and its inhibitive display policy. As the foremost exhibiting body in Britain, it had, for a number of years, concentrated on the display of paintings by established Academicians despite the fact that their ambit included designs for the decorative arts. Keen to publicise such partiality and to demonstrate the development of a much wider scope of artistic endeavour, the Arts and Crafts Exhibition Society was set up to provide a democratically organised, regular display of the fine and applied arts. Many members of the Society adopted Morris's philosophies on design and manufacture and, within a few years of the first exhibition in November 1888 at the New Gallery, Regent Street in London, industrial and craft work achieved a unity of purpose not experienced before. Encouraged by such comradeship and common purpose, and a new enthusiasm towards improving the design and construction of the decorative arts, Britain saw the development of a new artistic movement – one of the most original seen for centuries.

However, to believe that all artefacts associated with the Movement over the following twenty years were made under the same improved and enlightened conditions is misguided. Similarly, no one discernible style is identifiable in the work of the main exponents. Nevertheless, by looking more closely at the designs of the period a similar underlying character can be identified. But what are the elements which contribute towards this essentially very British form of decoration? Why did it become so popular abroad and why has it remained such an important contributing force behind domestic and commercial production to this day? To try to answer these questions a closer look at the prevailing styles and pattern types associated with the Arts and Crafts Movement is necessary.

EASTERN ECLECTICISM

From the 1860s, Eastern patterns dominated the design of British decorative arts and the first Arts and Crafts Exhibition reflected this passion. Three of the four textile manufacturers involved – Morris & Company, Thomas Wardle of Leek in Staffordshire and Turnbull and Stockdale of Stubbins in Lancashire – all displayed fabrics influenced by Japanese, Indian, Middle or Near Eastern art. Subsequent exhibitions showed a continuation of this trend in textiles and other forms of production. Some designers and manufacturers were more susceptible to foreign patterns than others. The ceramicist William de Morgan favoured Persian colourings and motifs for his pottery and tiles (22) and Lewis F. Day, one of the most commercially successful of decorative designers, used both Japanese (27, 46a) and Turkish motifs in his early designs (46b). The textile printer, Thomas Wardle, was particularly interested in Indian patterns. He travelled widely through the East and imported and copied many of the patterns he saw on his travels. The Leek Embroidery Society, founded by his wife Elizabeth, used Wardle's prints as the ground pattern over which they embroidered (36a). This helped develop a trend for so-called "Anglo-Indian" work.

This eclecticism in design proved very important in shaping the styles of the later Movement. Designers and manufacturers gained confidence from studying traditional forms and this awareness of the success and versatility of ancient patterns encouraged greater originality in their own work, once the fashion for copying such things had subsided. In a number of cases such ideas continued to be used well into the twentieth century (49).

THE INFLUENCE OF GARDEN DESIGN

Despite a preoccupation with geometric, architectural patterns in the middle of the nineteenth century, the Arts and Crafts Movement saw a revival of interest in natural forms and these provided the single most important source of inspiration for designers. This followed a radical change in fashions affecting the domestic garden. Various publications from the early 1880s advocated a more natural garden layout in order to exploit the individual characteristics of the British countryside and reflect the natural effects of the seasons. The garden became an important part of the design of new houses, and lawns and herbaceous borders an integral part of the plans of most of the leading architects of the day. A number of architects including A.H. Mackmurdo (1851–1942), (38b), Charles Harrison Townsend (1851–1928), (42b) and C.F.A. Voysey (1857–1941), (see especially 52b, 56b, 56a) also produced patterns for wallpapers and textiles and, not surprisingly, similar ideas soon proliferated in the decorative arts.

Other designers and manufacturers were keen amateur gardeners. Lindsay P. Butterfield (1869–1948) used his fine draughtsmanship to exploit his love of flowers and keen botanical knowledge (54a, 66, 60b, 60a, 64, Oslo), whereas the manufacturer George Percival Baker, a notable plant collector, chose to buy designs which included his favourite plants (51b, 63, 66, 60b, 60a, 64b, 64a).

Designs did not always show instantly recognisable floral subjects and stylisations of flowers and plants were used in various forms, for embroidery (32a, 31, to 36b), wallpapers (29, 30, 24b), and printed and woven textiles. Fabric designs produced by the Silver Studio and, in particular Harry Napper (1860–1940), one of their most outstanding designers, often show quite eccentric forms based on flowers (40b, 41a, 40a). Alternatively, Lewis F. Day (1845–1910) (28, 51a), and George Haité (1851–1924) (38a, 51b) produced both realistic and innovative flower patterns throughout their careers. Despite the Continental fashion for sinuous inanimate designs (now universally labelled Art Nouveau), this had only a slight effect on the work of British designers (53a, 66b) and the increase of trade between Europe and Britain was a direct result of the popularity of British work, rather than the other way around.

FIGURATIVE DESIGNS

Flowers and trees were not the only motifs used in Arts and Crafts patterns and figurative designs also played an important role. Walter Crane (1845–1915), the most prominent founder member and first President of the Arts and Crafts Exhibition Society, was a notable book illustrator and many of his designs show his ability in this field. Apart from a few floral patterns (26, 37, 55, 57) his work often incorporates classical (25) or allegorical figures (23, 47). Despite designing for many different forms of the decorative arts, the style of his repeating designs was never controlled by technqiue. This is exemplified in many of his textile and wallpaper designs which are very similar in form, their only differences showing in the positing borders (25, 47). Herbert Horne (1864–1916), also used figures for some of his early eccentric designs which were worked while he was still a member of the short-lived yet influential Century Guild (45). However, his highly imaginative and attractive later designs for wallpapers (29), textiles and particularly embroideries, rely on the use of floral forms. C.F.A. Voysey's designs of animals and birds are now thought by many to epitomise the Arts and Crafts style and it is true to say that from the 1880s to the 1930s he was the most influential of all British designers. His highly original drawings illustrate all the vital elements of good design, incorporating interesting and often unusual subjects, beautifully drawn and attractively coloured. Although not the only Arts and Crafts designer to use bird patterns, these proliferated in Voysey's work and another important aspect of the British countryside was brought from the garden into the home. His birds showed many stylised and simplified forms (44, 41b, 50b, 52b, 56b, 56a, 61) and his designs were easily adapted to all printing and weaving techniques. Crane and the artists of the Silver Studio (68b, 55 and 52a) also drew a number of bird designs but none were as close to Voysey's style as Godfrey Blount's embroidered linen panels worked by the Haslemere Peasant Industries (31).

COMMERCIAL MANUFACTURE

The importance of the Arts and Crafts Movement in establishing a return to workshop practices and the revival of traditional techniques is already well established. Of equal historical significance was the improvement in design and manufacture of mass-produced goods. The crucial part played by manufacturers in bringing about this change should not be underestimated. The successful practical manifestations of the Movement owe a great deal not only to their entrepreneurial skills but also to their foresight in employing free-lance designers and their sensitivity in transcribing their designs.

During the latter part of the nineteenth century the nature of fashionable furnishings changed with the modernisation and development of long-established firms and the opening of various small concerns specialising in the production of particular goods or types of decoration. Most of these enlightened workshops and factories, whether new or old, adopted techniques which would produce fashionable effects such as printed velveteens (48b, 74b, 75), woven double cloths (43b, 39b, 44, 39a, 43a, 42a), appliqué embroidery (31), discharged block-printing (53b, 51a) and stencilling (24b). By combining these with the best designs available they not only guaranteed their own success but also helped to improve the professional status of free-lance designers. The identification of both designer and maker of all items exhibited in the Arts and Crafts Exhibitions also provided a considerable breakthrough as manufacturers had previously been reluctant to identify the source of their designs. As their reputations now depended to some extent on the patterns they used, many entered business agreements with designers to produce a certain number of exclusive drawings each year. For instance, Alexander Morton signed contracts with both Voysey and Butterfield and L.F. Day acted as artistic director for the fabric printers Turnbull and Stockdale for a number of years.

IMPROVEMENTS IN EDUCATION

Never had the reputation of the decorative artist been so high, and the foundation of such organisations as the Society of Designers attested to this new importance. Fortunately, many of the most successful free-designers also undertook part-time teaching, subsequently passing on their talents to future generations of art students.

Domestically worked techniques, such as embroidery, also benefitted from an improvement in teaching methods and various colleges became associated with styles and particular techniques. Classes under the tutelage of talented craftswomen such as May Morris (19), Annie Jack (32a, 32b) Lousia Pesel (36b) and Grace Christie (35) advocated the revival of traditional techniques, whereas an entirely new approach to the craft was encouraged in Scotland. Experimental, stylised embroideries completed under Jessie Newbery and Ann Macbeth (34b, 34a) at the Glasgow School of Art are now internationally famous because of their association with Charles Rennie Mackintosh. However, it was only many years later that Mackintosh and other notable Glasgow designers produced commercial patterns themselves (67b, 67a).

THE INFLUENCE OF BRITISH DESIGNERS ABROAD

International exhibitions provided designers and manufacturers with the greatest opportunities to publicise their work outside Britain. The Arts and Crafts Exhibition also became an important shop window for visiting foreigners and subsequently many British designers, craftsmen and companies became known throughout Europe and America. Such individuals as Walter Crane established their international reputations as early as 1876 (with exhibits at the Philadelphia Centennial Exposition), whereas the greatest period of Britain's influence abroad dated from the 1890s, and covers the period in which the Arts and Crafts Movement flourished. This influence showed not only in large purchases of designs and products by foreign manufacturers and shops but also in the patterning and manner of production adopted in foreign workshops. The French were particularly impressed by these new patterns and as well as two of Paris's most artistic shops (Liberty & Co and Bing's Maison de L'Art Nouveau) stocking British products, manufacturers also became interested in British patterns. Alsatian printers (48b) and the weavers Vanoutryve and Leborgne, both of Lille, bought many designs (40b, 41a). Similarly, British work influenced established French designers and manufacturers (77, 78b, 80).

The popularity of British commercial designs can be traced throughout Europe and American and Scandinavian collections today (69a, 69b, 71–76b). Although some items were bought in London most were purchased in European shops such as Hirschwald's Hohenzoller Kaufhaus in Berlin (71–73, 74a–76b) and Steen and Strøm in Christiania – now Oslo – (74b).

American shops were also keen to retail British goods, and a few commercial companies produced patterns in the British style (70). However, the influence of the British Arts and Crafts Movement was much more deeply felt in America and manifested itself almost exclusively in the production of hand-crafted items. More faithfully following the philosophies of Morris and his followers than many of their British counterparts, these craftsmen developed these ideas in a new and original way.

Linda Parry
A Curator, Department of
Textile Furnishing and Dress,
The Victoria and Albert Museum, London

[15]

Textiles of the American Arts and Crafts Movement

When the Arts and Crafts movement crossed the Atlantic Ocean to the United States, several aspects changed, or at least took on a different emphasis. The American movement both developed after the British one was well established and continued later into the twentieth century. In Britain the First World War was undoubtedly a factor in putting an abrupt and definitive end to the movement. In the States, the war did not interrupt the pattern of domestic life as dramatically as it did in England, allowing the movement to continue for a longer length of time.

The Arts and Crafts movement occurred at a time when Americans were insecure about their own tastes in terms of design. Most Americans felt that European products and designs adapted from seventeenth and eighteenth century examples were preferable to contemporary American work. The decorator and designer Candace Wheeler observed[1] that although silk weaving was practised in the States, patterned fabrics were copied from textiles made in other countries and were sold as English or French rather than American.

One of the major differences in the two countries as far as textiles are concerned, was the role taken by manufacturers. In the United States most manufacturers of patterned fabric were not readily prepared to produce new designs for the higher priced market. They preferred to copy or adapt a design which had already proven to be successful. Wallpaper manufacturers, on the other hand, seemed more willing to use American designers.

Englishmen were often quoted on the subject of design in the American book and magazine press. The names of John Ruskin and William Morris were frequently evoked, sometimes incorrectly. Oscar Wilde, C.R. Ashbee and Walter Crane, all Englishmen who had visited the States, had both influenced and perhaps

1. Candace Wheeler, *Yesterdays in a Busy Life*, Harper & Brothers, 1918, New York, p.236.

[16]

in turn been influenced by Americans. Eventually both Ruskin's point of view – that of copying directly from nature – and the point of view of Christopher Dresser, William Morris and Henry Cole – that of abstracting flat pattern from nature – were seen in American products. Often the same person or organization did both types of designs. For example, textiles designed by Associated Artists, and by the Deerfield designers Margaret Whiting and Ellen Miller, could be either simple drawings of familiar plants put into repeat, or stylized and abstracted designs. Flat areas of abstracted pattern were often found on the walls of a home, on commercially prepared wallpapers and in stencilled designs.

The American response to the Arts and Crafts movement was neither a mirror image of the British movement nor a colonization. The movement took its own form. The United States was a much younger country and was in a different stage of its own development, historically and economically. The exhortation, from design reformers, to look around oneself and to take inspiration from nature delighted most Americans with its implications of freedom and independence, and vaguely disturbed them because of their lack of self confidence in design issues.

From the beginning there were confusions and contradictions both with what the style looked like and with the various philosophies associated with the movement. The rhetoric of the social reformers and the guidelines of Arts and Crafts exhibition juries were often contradictory. A devotion to the abstract ideal of beauty did not always correlate with social responsibility. Romantic ideals about the artist/craftsman often did not fit with reality. And, an essential contradiction, that while mass-produced objects can be marketed at low cost, few handmade products are within the reach of people with a moderate income, was never surmounted.

It was difficult for manufacturers who were interested in maximum profits to incorporate social reform within the factory. Yet they wished to have the Arts and Crafts consumer as a customer. Thus a number of products were created for the Arts and Crafts consumer under factory conditions that did not meet with the Arts and Crafts ideal.

Just as in Britain, the movement existed for many years before it received the name "Arts and Crafts", and that phrase was not always adopted enthusiastically. "Craftsman" and "Mission Style" were two other frequently used terms. In the United States the term Arts and Crafts became associated with the individual working at home and with the societies formed as exhibitions and sales organizations rather than with manufacturers.

Within the Arts and Crafts societies many individuals worked on small, non-essential decorative objects such as wastepaper baskets or embroideries from a kit, feeling they were involved with design reform. Handwork, while absorbing of creative energies, rarely produced much income, causing it to become a leisure activity or hobby. By the early 1920s most of the practitioners must have realized that the ideal of the craftsman, in terms of forming self-supporting communities of artists and craftsmen, was impossible in an industrialized society. Yet the work of individual craftspeople, working from their own studios, continued.

The domestic nature of the movement was always important. Products were designed for the home, the writings of the period put emphasis upon creating beautiful and simple domestic surroundings and much of the work there was done by females. The home itself was to make a statement about ideals of beauty and simplicity. In the American movement a number of the best known names were women: Candace Wheeler, Margaret Whiting, Ellen Miller, Lydia Bush-Brown and many of the ceramicists such as Adelaide Alsop Robineau.

It is curious to note that textiles per se were not very important in American Arts and Crafts interiors. Both the architecture and the furniture were meant to dominate the look of a room with their prominent use of wood and their strong horizontals and verticals. Yet textiles were extremely important in the growth of the movement. The techniques of embroidery, appliqué, stencilling and block printing provided an opportunity for individual expression within the reach of the average person who had some creative ability and a desire to participate in beautifying their own surroundings. Many textile products were one-of-a-kind pieces, not production work.

William Morris's products appealed to Americans. By the 1880s Morris fabrics and wallpapers were available for sale in many of the larger cities in the States. In Chicago, Morris fabrics were used in 1886 in the lavish and imposing house which H.H. Richardson designed for John Glessner and his family. John Glessner later wrote that the pattern on one of the silks was drawn by Morris himself and that much of the embroidery was done by Mrs. Glessner[2].

Early examples of the thinking found in the Arts and Crafts movement were seen in the work of Associated Artists, founded

2. John Glessner, *The Story of a House* 1923, reprinted in *The House at 1800 Prairie Avenue* published by The Glessner House, Chicago, Illinois, 1978.

in 1879 by Louis Comfort Tiffany (1848–1933), Samuel Colman (1832–1920), Lockwood de Forest (1850–1932) and Candace Wheeler (1828–1923) as an interior decorating firm. In her autobiography, *Yesterdays in a busy Life*, Candace Wheeler quotes Tiffany as saying to her, "We are going after the money there is in art but art is there all the same"[3]. Within the organization it was Mrs. Wheeler who was in charge of choosing and supplying the woven textiles and embroideries. In 1883 the partnership dissolved so that each member could pursue his or her own interests. Mrs. Wheeler kept the name, Associated Artists, using the argument that she had thought it up in the first place. Tiffany took the name "Tiffany Associates". Along with his well known work in glass, he continued to decorate interiors, including many churches.

Between 1883 and 1907 the association was run by Candace Wheeler, one of her daughters and later by one of her sons. The Associated Artists designed, printed and wove textiles, many of which were produced by the firm of Cheney Brothers in South Manchester, Connecticut (82–86). Several members of the Cheney family and the Wheeler family were close friends and the professional relationship may have developed out of the personal relationship.

Associated Artists worked with Frank and Knight Cheney to use patterns drawn by American designers, many taken from very familiar and easily recognizable plants, for printed and woven fabrics. The printed fabrics can be identified by a monogram of a double capital letter A incorporated within the design (83, 84a, 84b) but the monogram was not included in the woven fabrics. Some of the Associated Artists fabrics were used in the Mark Twain house in Hartford, Connecticut, and in Andrew Carnegie's house in the Berkshires.

The reasons why the firm closed in 1907 remain unclear. It does not appear as if there was a continuation of the work by another parallel organization. But Candace Wheeler's ideas, those of using the simple and familiar as design sources and creating practical products, reached into another generation by her teaching at Cooper Union and by her writings in women's magazines and in books.

One of the best known and most successful examples of a number of small societies which sprang up around the country in response to the desire for design reform was the one in Deerfield, Massachusetts. In 1896 the Society of Blue and White Needlework was started by Ellen Miller (1854–1929) and Margaret Whiting

3. Wheeler, ibid. p.232.

[19]

(1860–1946), both residents of Deerfield, a small town in the northwestern part of the state. At first the society adapted designs found on eighteenth century embroideries in Massachusetts, embroidering with blue and white yarns on white foundation cloth. But within a few years they were embroidering with multi-colored yarns on colored cloths and had added the technique of appliqué to their work (85a). They also began to use contemporary designs. Subtle toning and unexpected color combinations became associated with this group.

A capital letter 'D' within a spinning wheel, the trademark of the society, was embroidered on each piece the Society of Blue and White Needlework completed. Often the trademark was cleverly incorporated into the design and is not immediately visible (85a). Nothing but finished work was sold by the society even though there were requests for both stamped fabrics which the purchaser could embroider and for the dyed yarns. Work of the society was often shown in Arts and Crafts exhibitions in cities such as Boston, New York, and Chicago, and the society received favorable press attention.

Margaret Whiting, who had stated that she had founded her society on principles set down by Ruskin[4] clearly saw the confusion which resulted when social reform was combined with design reform. "Village industries are menaced by the danger of confusing social reform with craftsmanship. It is not charity but art which founds and maintains a craft."[5] The society continued in operation until 1926 when the deaths of some members and the failing eyesight of others caused it to close.

In 1901 Gustave Stickley (1858–1942), who operated the Craftsman Workshops for furniture just outside Syracuse, New York, started a magazine, *The Craftsman*. The magazine contained articles of interest to the Arts and Crafts community and has come to be widely quoted and cited. Articles included a discussion of William Morris by Irene Sargent, an examination of Stickley's home and Craftsman workshops, home training in woodwork, articles on the American Indian, and on California's contribution to a national architecture.

The Craftsman shops first sold furniture and metalwork but the firm also sold imported and domestic textiles. Rugs came from Ireland and India and American textiles were available as well. Stamped embroideries in the form of kits for the purchaser to

4. Margaret Miller, "The Deerfield Society", *Modern Priscilla* Vol. XV, No.5, July 1901, p.1.
5. quoted in Margery Howe, *Deerfield Embroidery*, Charles Scribner, 1976, New York, p.21.

complete were among the products available at Craftsman shops. In all the Stickley furniture, structure and the grain of the wood was important. It was intended that the furniture be used with textiles which conveyed the same robust and strong quality. Stickley adherents favored table runners and cushions made of linen or jute where the weave of the foundation cloth was apparent. Designs for these articles often appeared in *The Craftsman* (88).

Batik was a textile craft to which Americans responded enthusiastically within this period. The craft consisted in drawing on cloth with wax, then immersing the fabric in dyes which resisted the waxed areas. Batik had been brought to the Netherlands from the Dutch East Indies and spread to other parts of Europe. Early in the twentieth century the Dutch artist Peter Mijer brought the technique to the United States. Mijer collaborated with American artists and wrote a book outlining the technique[6].

In the 1910s and 1920s batik was frequently practised in the eastern half of the United States. A reviewer wrote of an 1917 exhibition in New York, "The majority of the exhibits are in batik which appears to have fascinated the whole artistic population of Greenwich Village and the outlying provinces of New York's Bohemian world"[7]. Artists such as Arthur Crisp and Lydia Bush-Brown (90a and 90b) produced large hangings used as wall decorations in homes and hotels and other public spaces. Shawls and articles of wearing apparel were also made. Art magazines such as Amy Mali Hicks's "Batik, its making and its use" showed examples of the work and shelter magazines spread the craft to a wider audience.[8]

Lydia Bush-Brown (1887–1984) trained as a decorative artist at Pratt Institute in Brooklyn, New York. In her youth she travelled extensively in Europe and in the Middle East, always making sketches of the country in which she was staying. When she returned to the States she studied principles of dyeing with Charles Pellow, a chemist at Columbia University. Using batik she made dresses, cloaks and scarves to order and then made larger batik hangings for the walls of residences and offices. Her very poetic approach to her subjects was always apparent.

She worked on commission, repeating her designs in different color schemes if a customer wished it. Her batiks were shown in

6. Pieter Mijer, *Batiks and How to Make Them*, Dodd Mead & Company, 1919, New York.
7. ——— "Textile Exhibition of the Art Alliance of America, *Good Furniture*, July 1917, pp.6/7.
8. Amy Maili Hicks, "Batik, its making and its use", *House & Garden*, November 1913, pp.289, 290, 318.

galleries and in exhibitions and were often illustrated in magazines where they were favorably described[9]. In 1923 she was awarded the Medal of Honor by the Boston Arts and Crafts Society.

The textile techniques of block printing (91a and 91b) and stencilling were not only practised by artists but also were explained in a how-to-do-it format to the interested in magazines such as *American Homes and Gardens* and *The House Beautiful*[10]. Block printing and stencilling on fabric were crafts that the aware homeowner could be expected to use for him or herself. Yet how much block printing and stencilling was done by people who had not gone to art school remains an unanswered question.

Art schools and art classes began to appear in greater number across the entire country. The art school of the H. Sophie Newcomb Memorial College in New Orleans, Louisiana, began in 1894 with pottery and later expanded to include the crafts of weaving (92), embroidery, metalwork and bookbinding. The products and the name of the school were known nationally because of the number of exhibitions which the school entered.

As a way of life the Arts and Crafts movement failed to live up to the visionary ideals of its early adherents; much of the work shown at their exhibitions lacked the elements of good design and the phrase itself gradually acquired a pejorative tone.

But the Arts and Crafts movement as it existed in this country at the turn of the century left a legacy: the work of individual craftsmen improved: in the years after the First World War a number of craftspeople such as Lydia Bush-Brown and Edith Huntington Snow (d.1960) (93) set up their own studios and produced well made products of good design.

Gillian Moss
Assistant Curator of Textiles
Cooper-Hewitt Museum
The Smithsonian Institution's
National Museum of Design
New York

9. For example, Babette Becker, "Silk Murals of Lydia Bush-Brown", *The American Magazine of Art*, 1928, pp.556–560.
10. Harry E. Wood "Block Printing", *The House Beautiful*, April 1905, pp.21/22.
Mabel Tuke Priestman "How to make and apply Stencils", *American Homes and Gardens*, February 1906, pp.104/106.

The Plates

Please note that when there are two
images on a page, the captions refer as follows:
top (a), bottom (b) or left (a), right (b)

PLATE 1

Stained-glass panel, depicting a woman. Designed by Ford Madox Brown and William Morris and executed by Morris c.1860. The decoration on the clothing and dense floral background shows Morris's early interest in pattern making.

PLATE 2a

Original design for Vine *wallpaper drawn by William Morris in 1873. Watercolour and pencil. The design is marked with instructions for the block cutters.*

PLATE 2b

Original pencil and watercolour design for Rose *printed fabric. Drawn by William Morris and registered on December 8th 1883. Both cotton and linen grounds were used with indigo discharge printing to achieve this design in which most of the ground was bleached out.*

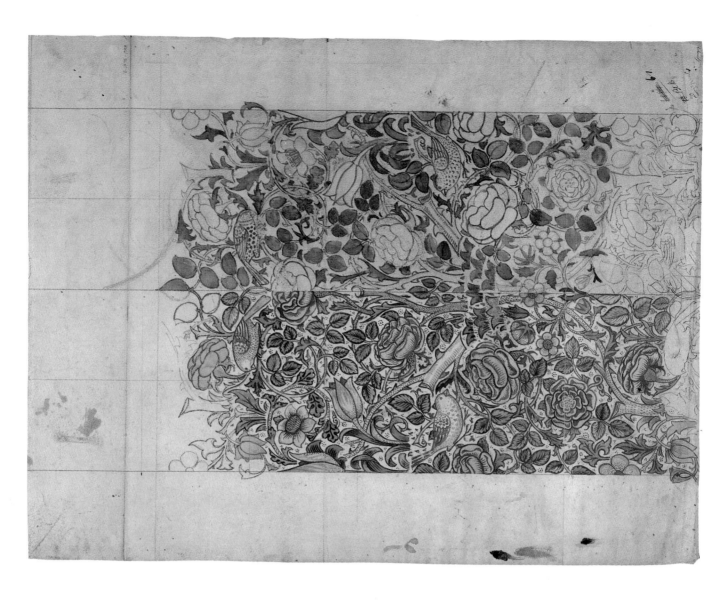

PLATE 3

Fruit or Pomegranate *block-printed wallpaper. Designed by William Morris in 1862 and printed by Jeffrey & Co. in distemper colours.*

PLATE 4a

Crown Imperial *woven cotton fabric. Designed by Morris and registered on November 18th 1876. One of Morris's earliest woven designs. The cloth was woven by the Bradford firm of Dixon, Morris & Co. not having the facilities at this time to weave this type of fabric. The design was also used in a larger version as a woollen cloth.*

PLATE 4b

Marigold *block-printed cotton. Designed by William Morris as a wallpaper and registered on April 15th 1875. Printed by Thomas Wardle of Leek, as with all Morris designs produced before 1881.*

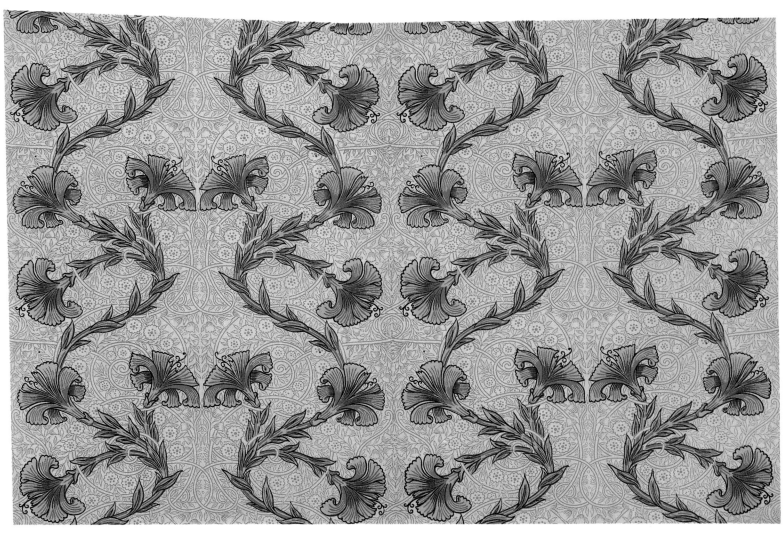

PLATE 5

Jasmine block-printed wallpaper, designed by William Morris in 1872. Morris's knowledge of garden plants is shown in the life-like manner in which the plant curves and in the delicacy of the flowers.

PLATE 6a

Carnation *block-printed cotton. Registered on October 15th 1875 and possibly designed for Morris & Co. by Kate Faulkner, a friend of the Morris family who provided the firm with designs for tiles and wallpapers.*

PLATE 6b

Lea *block-printed and indigo discharged cotton. Designed by William Morris and registered on February 2nd 1885. Together with all other designs made after 1881, this fabric was printed at Morris & Co.'s Merton Abbey Works.*

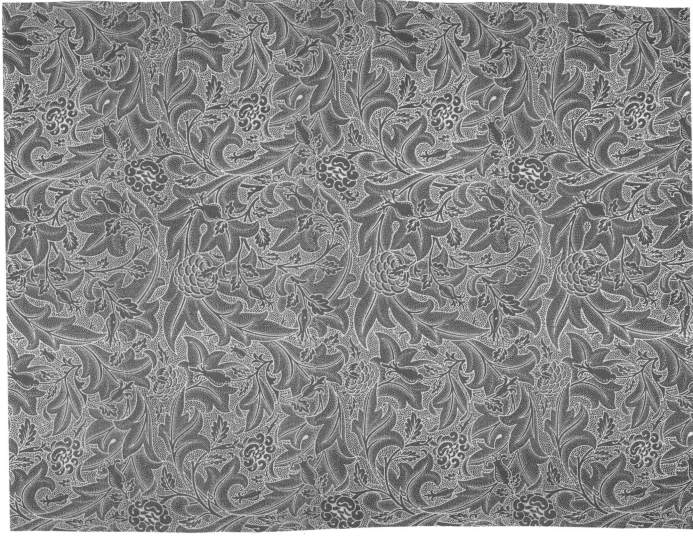

PLATE 7

Linoleum or, as Morris & Co. described it, Corticine floor cloth. *Designed by Morris in 1875, this proved popular with clients and despite a number of examples surviving, only one pattern is known.*

PLATE 8a

Artichoke *machine-woven Kidderminster carpeting. Designed by William Morris between 1875 and 1880. Manufactured for Morris & Co. by the Heckmondwike Manufacturing Company of Yorkshire.*

PLATE 8b

Tulip and Lily *machine-woven Kidderminster carpeting. Designed by William Morris about 1875 and woven for Morris & Co. by the Heckmondwike Manufacturing Company. The carpet was also available with a matching border.*

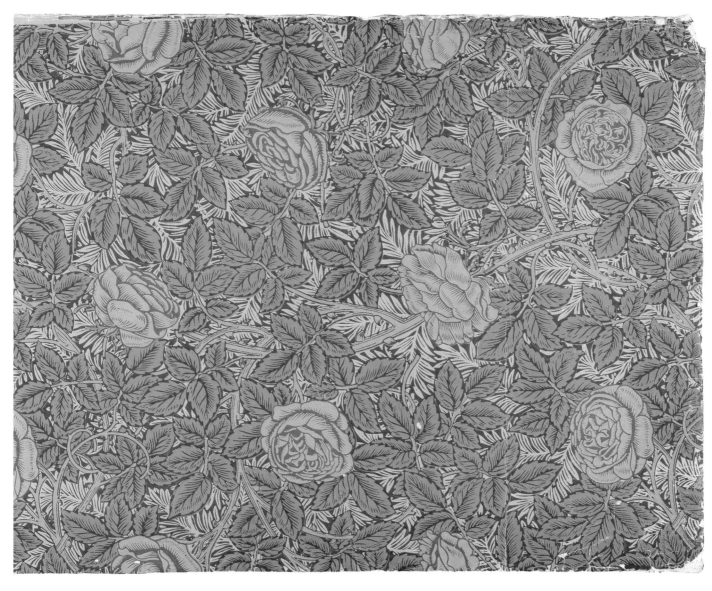

PLATE 11

Acanthus embroidered coverlet. Designed by William Morris about 1880 and embroidered by his daughter May Morris in silks on a woollen ground. One of a number of known versions. The composition of this cover shows Morris's preoccupation with carpet designing at this time.

PLATE 12a

Eden *block-printed cotton. Designed by Henry Dearle about 1905. One of Dearle's later patterns based on Turkish and Persian silks and carpets in the South Kensington Museum.*

PLATE 12b

Honeysuckle *block-printed linen. Designed by William Morris and registered on October 11th 1876. The design was printed by Thomas Wardle onto a number of grounds including tusser silk, velveteen, and challis (silk and wool) but only cottons and linens were produced in marketable quantities.*

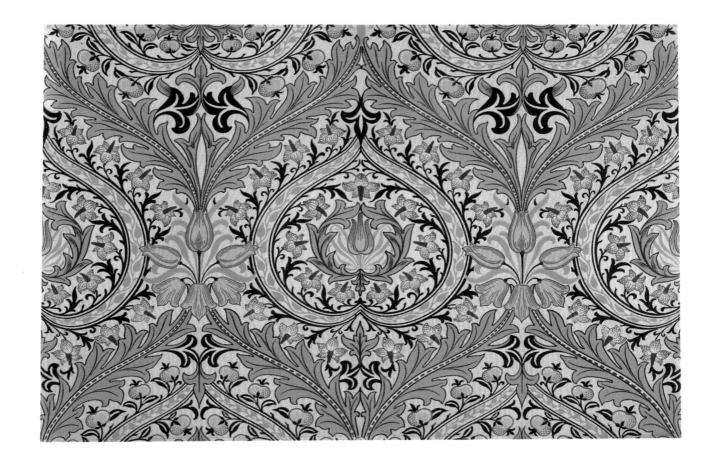

PLATE 13

Original watercolour design for Redcar *carpet. Drawn by Morris between 1879 and 1881. The design shows a quarter of the entire scheme.*

PLATE 14a

Tulip *woven woollen fabric, designed by Henry Dearle between 1895 and 1900. One of Dearle's most confident and successful designs in which he transcended the strong Morris influence of his early years.*

PLATE 14b

Vine and Pomegranate *three-ply woven woollen fabric. Probably designed by Kate Faulkner for Morris & Co. about 1877. This heavy type of fabric proved very popular with the firm's clients and was used for both curtaining and floorcovering.*

PLATE 15

Redcar hand-knotted Hammersmith carpet. Designed by William Morris for the Bell family's house, Red Barns in Redcar, Yorkshire (now Cleveland). This is the second version of the design woven by Morris & Co. in the early 20th century.

PLATE 16a

Pots of Flowers *indigo discharged and block-printed cotton. Designed by William Morris as a lining fabric and registered on October 18th 1883. Originally printed at Merton Abbey onto a reduced width so that full pieces would provide the lining to heavy woollen curtains.*

PLATE 16b

Eyebright *indigo discharged and block-printed cotton. One of three small scale designs made by Morris to be used for linings although later used for general purposes, including dress. The pattern was registered on November 23rd 1883.*

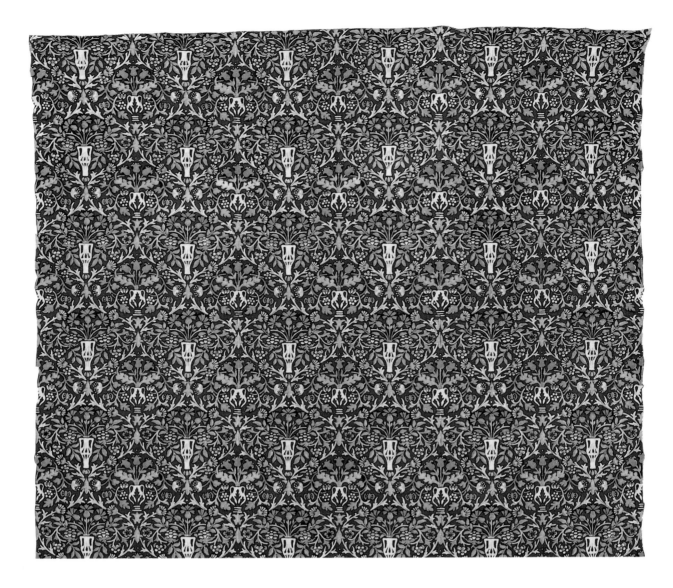

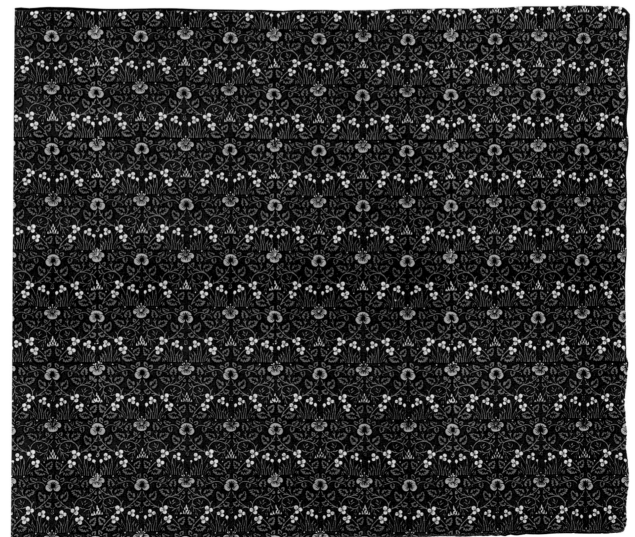

PLATE 17

The Owl embroidered portière. Designed by Henry Dearle about 1890 and worked in silks on a woven silk damask ground by Mrs Battye. The design, background cloth and embroidery silks were all supplied by the Morris shop in Oxford Street.

PLATE 18a

Orchard machine-printed wallpaper designed by Henry Dearle in the 1890s. The pattern is similar to designs Dearle made for embroideries. The curving acanthus leaf shows his continuing interest in motifs originally favoured by Morris.

PLATE 18b

Arbutus wallpaper. Designed by Kathleen Kersey for Morris & Co. Machine reprinted by Sanderson & Sons. The designer produced a number of patterns for the firm although only the wallpapers are now identifiable. Her clean, crisp style helped to update Morris & Co.'s rather old fashioned reputation in the early 20th century.

PLATE 19

The Orchard *embroidered hanging. Designed by May Morris and embroidered under her supervision in the Morris workshops for her friend Theodosia Middlemore. Another panel of this design was exhibited at the 1890 Arts and Crafts Exhibition.*

PLATE 20a

Helena *woven silk and wool double cloth. Designed by Henry Dearle about 1890 and woven for Morris & Co. by Alexander Morton & Co. of Darvel. One of two Morris & Co. designs woven in this type of cloth, Morton's went on to adopt the technique for its own retail use.*

PLATE 20b

Brocatel *woven silk and woollen fabric. Exhibited at the first Arts and Crafts Exhibition of 1888, it is likely that both Morris and Henry Dearle had a hand in its design. A sumptuous yet stiff fabric, it proved highly suitable for use on walls in grand decorative schemes.*

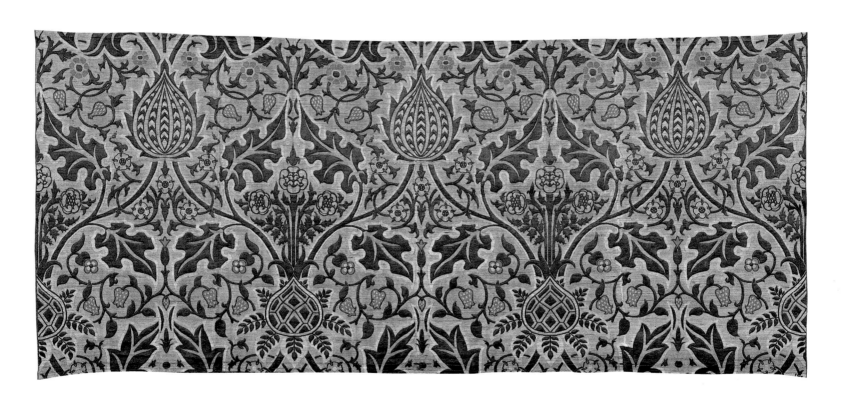

PLATE 21a

Seaweed *wallpaper. One of Dearle's most successful designs for Morris &
Co. originally hand-printed by Jeffrey & Co. in the late 19th century. This is
a later machine printed example, by Sanderson & Sons, Jeffrey & Co's
successors.*

PLATE 21b

Tom Tit *wallpaper designed by Henry Dearle in the 1890s and machine-
printed by Jeffrey & Co. Dearle's early patterns are often imitative of
Morris's work and, although tighter in style, adapt well to this technique.*

PLATE 22

Tile *designed by William de Morgan, 1882–8. Earthenware painted in enamel colours.*

PLATE 23

Flower Fairies, *a group of six tiles after a design by Walter Crane. Probably manufactured by Pilkingtons about 1900.*

PLATE 24a

Block-printed wallpaper. Designed by Albert Moore and manufactured by Jeffrey & Co. in 1875. A rare design from this notable Victorian artist. The disposition of pattern and colouring anticipate the work of designers at the end of the 19th century.

PLATE 24b

Eltham *stencilled wallpaper. Produced by Shand Kydd Ltd. and probably designed by William Shand Kydd, the founder of the firm.*

PLATE 27

Pomegranate, *block-printed wallpaper. Designed by Lewis F. Day and manufactured by Jeffrey & Co, 1880–5.*

PLATE 28

Original pencil and watercolour design for The Magnolia *wallpaper.*
Drawn by Lewis F. Day in 1891 for Jeffrey & Co.

The "Magnolia"

Lewis F Day
1890

L F Day

PLATE 29

Original watercolour design by Herbert Percy Horne, 1886. Although assumed to be for wallpaper this pattern would also work successfully as a printed cotton.

PLATE 30

Lancaster Frieze block-printed wallpaper. Designed by William James Neatby and manufactured by Jeffrey & Co. from 1904. Neatby was chief designer for the wallpaper manufacturer, John Line & Sons, from 1907 and also designed tiles for Harrods' Food Hall.

PLATE 31

Embroidered Hanging designed by Godfrey Blount, 1896–7. Made by the Haslemere Peasant Industries using silks and applied hand-woven linens on a linen ground. The linens used were also produced at Haslemere.

PLATE 32a

Embroidered panel worked in wools on linen. Designed and made by Annie Jack in the 1890s. The wife of Morris & Co.'s chief furniture designer, her work is closely associated with the firm, especially with designs such as this where typical Morris motifs, such as pomegranates, are used.

PLATE 32b

Embroidered panel in wools on linen. Worked and probably designed by Annie Jack in the 1890s. Mrs Jack produced a number of embroideries using designs produced by herself and also by her husband, George.

PLATE 33

Details from a set of bed valances of embroidered and applied linens. Designed by Godfrey Blount and made in the workshops of the Haslemere Peasant Industries.

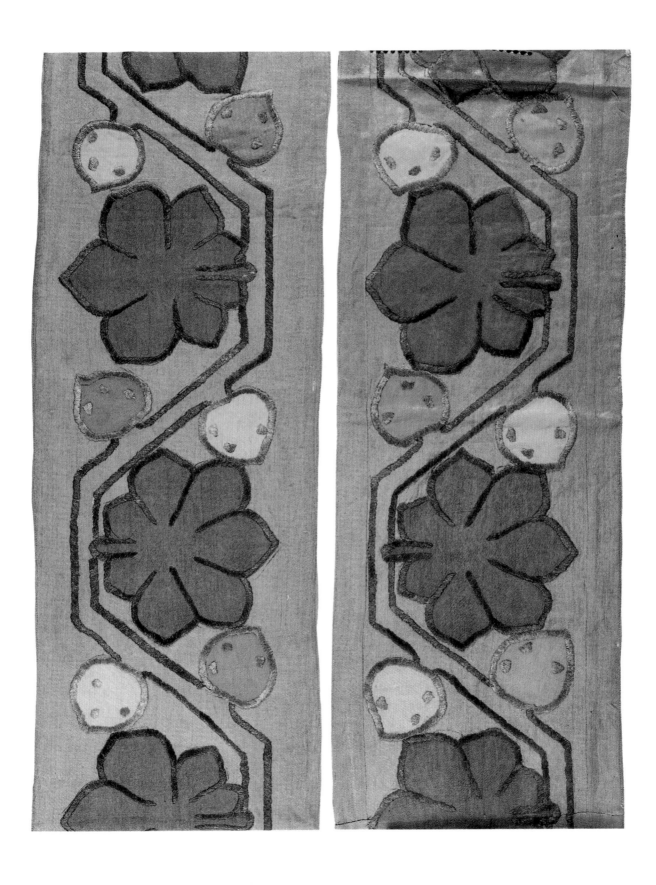

PLATE 34a

Detail of the corner of an embroidered tablecloth. Designed and worked by Ann Macbeth about 1900 in linens with silk embroidery. Most of the hand-woven linens used by Glasgow embroiderers were manufactured at the Lake District factory of Jonathan Harris & Sons.

PLATE 34b

Detail from an embroidered curtain. Designed and worked by Ann Macbeth about 1900. Linen with applied linen decoration, silk embroidery and beads.

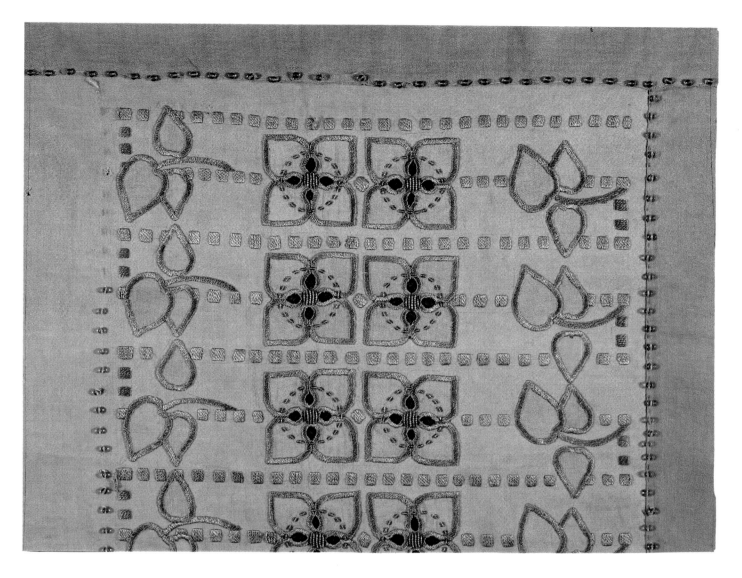

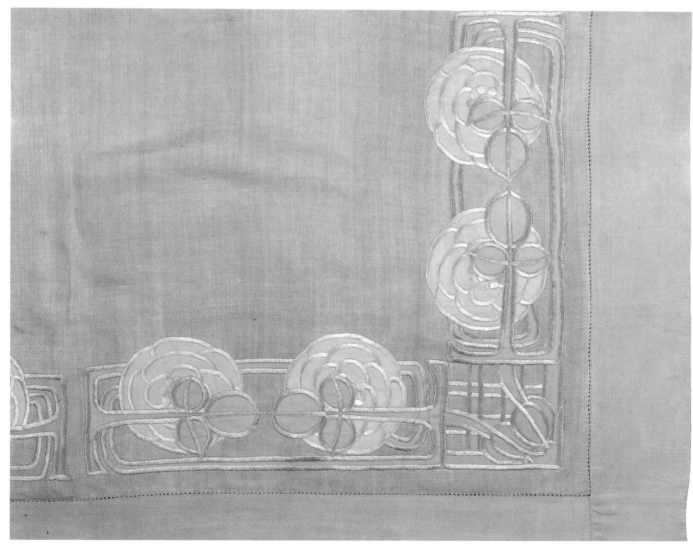

PLATE 35

*Embroidered panel designed and worked by Grace Christie about 1914.
Worked in silks on a linen ground. Mrs Christie's interest in the revival of
embroidery techniques is shown in the great variety of stitches used here.*

PLATE 36a

Panel of Leek Embroidery. *Embroidered in wools, silks, sequins and Japanese gold thread by Frances Mary Templeton in 1892. The panel is worked over the design of a block-printed silk manufactured by Thomas Wardle.*

PLATE 36b

Embroidered panel worked in silks on a linen ground. Adapted from a design by Louisa Pesel about 1900. Possibly made from a ready-printed kit.

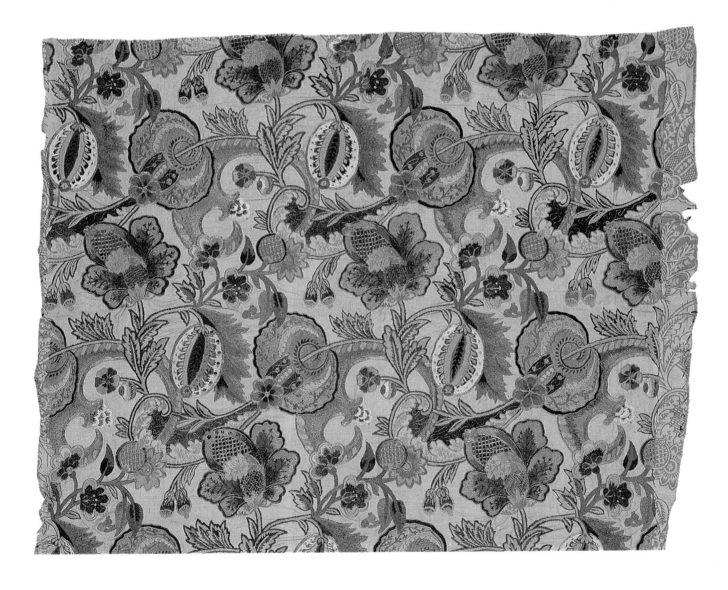

PLATE 37

Lily, Pink and Columbine *machine-woven Brussels carpeting. Designed by Walter Crane about 1895 and manufactured by J. Templeton of Glasgow.*

LILY PINK AND COLUMBINE
DESIGNED BY
WALTER CRANE

PLATE 38a

Woven woollen fabric designed by George C. Haité and manufactured by A.H. Lee & Sons from 1903. To achieve graduated colour, the surface of the cloth was block-printed after weaving.

PLATE 38b

Woven wool and cotton hanging designed by A.H. Mackmurdo. One of the first fabrics manufactured by A.H. Lee between 1887 and 1888 when he was manager of his father's factory in Bolton, Lancashire, and before he set up his own factory in Warrington.

PLATE 39a

Woven silk and wool double cloth designed by Lindsay P. Butterfield and manufactured from 1896 by Alexander Morton & Co. Most of Morton's double cloth weaves are reversible.

PLATE 39b

Woven silk and wool double cloth. Designed by Samuel Rowe and manufactured by A.H. Lee & Sons. Exhibited at the Arts and Crafts Exhibition of 1896.

PLATE 40a

Woven silk and woollen fabric designed by Harry Napper. Manufactured by J.W. & C. Ward of Halifax from September 1904.

PLATE 40b

Woven silk and cotton fabric. Designed by the Silver Studio between 1895 and 1900 and manufactured in Lille in Northern France.

PLATE 43a

Woven fabric of silk, cotton and cotton chenille. Manufactured by Alexander Morton & Co. about 1900. Possibly designed by Gavin Morton, nephew of Alexander Morton and head of the firm's studio from 1895–1908.

PLATE 43b

Woven silk, wool and cotton double cloth manufactured by Alexander Morton & Co. between 1900 and 1905. One of a large series of woven fabrics produced by this firm for Liberty's and other large fashionable shops.

PLATE 44

Purple Bird *woven silk and wool double cloth. Designed by C.F.A. Voysey in 1898, and manufactured by Alexander Morton & Co. who also manufactured a woven muslin of the same design. The name derives from the colouring of the original design.*

PLATE 45

The Angel with the Trumpet *block-printed. Designed by Herbert Horne for the Century Guild and printed by Simpson & Godlee from 1884.*

PLATE 46a

Block-printed velveteen designed by Lewis F. Day about 1888. Probably manufactured by Turnbull and Stockdale of Stubbins in Lancashire. Day was Artistic Director of the firm from 1881.

PLATE 46b

Block-printed velveteen designed by Lewis F. Day and printed by Thomas Wardle at Leek from 1888. The pattern shows Wardle's great interest in Turkish design. One of Wardle's Art Prints, the cloth was, almost certainly, sold through Wardle's shop in New Bond Street.

PLATE 47

The British Empire *or* The Colonies *roller-printed cotton. Designed by Walter Crane for the Royal Jubilee of 1887 and registered on May 20th of that year by the manufacturer Edmund Potter & Co.*

PLATE 48a

Block-printed silk. Drawn at the Silver Studio, the design was sold for four guineas in July 1897 to Thomas Wardle of Leek.

PLATE 48b

Block-printed velveteen designed by Arthur Silver, founder of the Silver Studio in 1896. Sold to Richard Stanway, a London warehouseman, the velveteen was printed in Mulhouse in France.

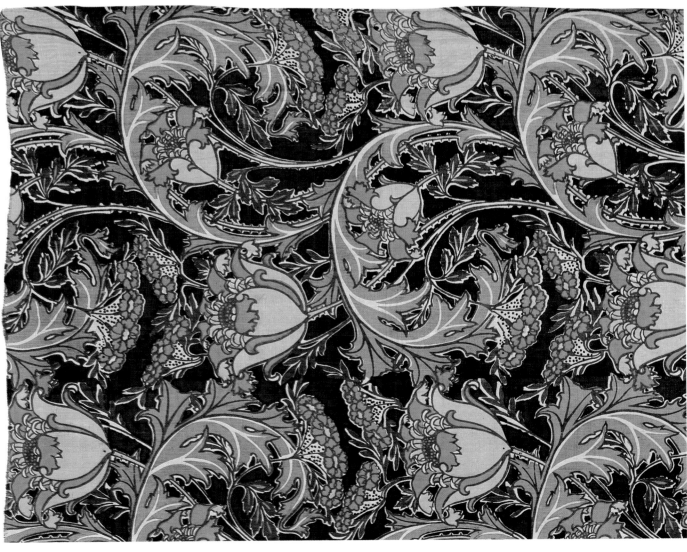

PLATE 49

Roller-printed cotton manufactured by F. Steiner & Co. in 1902. The pattern is strongly influenced by Japanese prints and was probably printed specifically for export to Europe.

PLATE 50a

Apple *block-printed linen. Designed by Lindsay P. Butterfield and manufactured by G.P. & J. Baker from about 1900.*

PLATE 50b

Saladin *roller-printed cotton designed by C.F.A. Voysey. Printed by Stead McAlpin for Warner & Sons in 1895.*

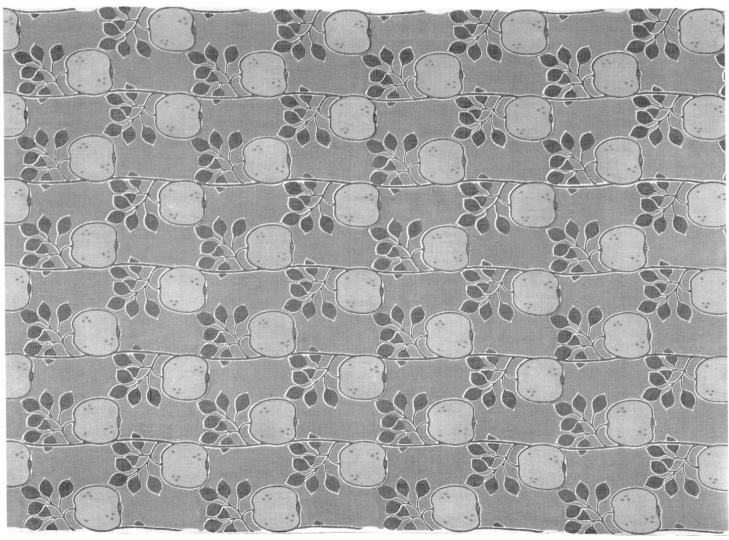

PLATE 51a

The New Dot *block-printed and indigo-discharged cotton. Designed by Lewis F. Day and manufactured by Turnbull and Stockdale from 1898.*

PLATE 51b

Harley *block-printed onto a cotton and linen figured ground, designed by George C. Haité and manufactured by G.P. & J. Baker from 1896.*

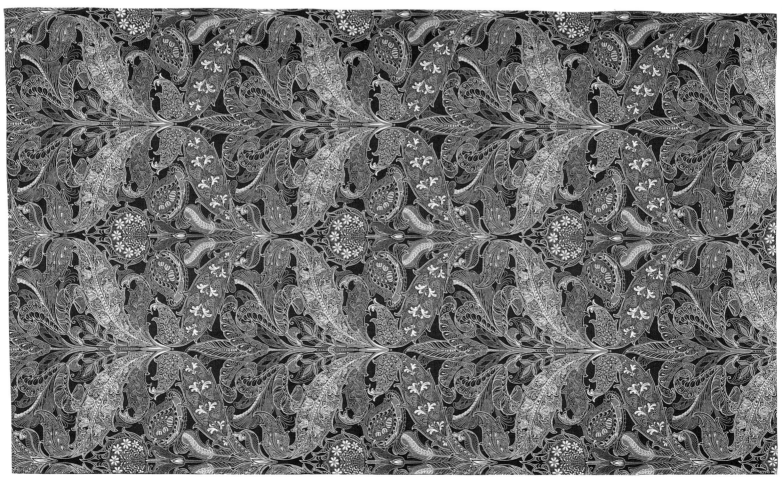

PLATE 52a

*Block-printed tusser silk. Designed by the Silver Studio about 1900 and
printed by Stead McAlpin & Co. of Carlisle for the Bradford firm of Denby.*

PLATE 52b

Hedgerow *block-printed linen. Designed by C.F.A Voysey and printed by
G.P. & J. Baker for the London furnishers Heal & Son, where it was sold
from 1908.*

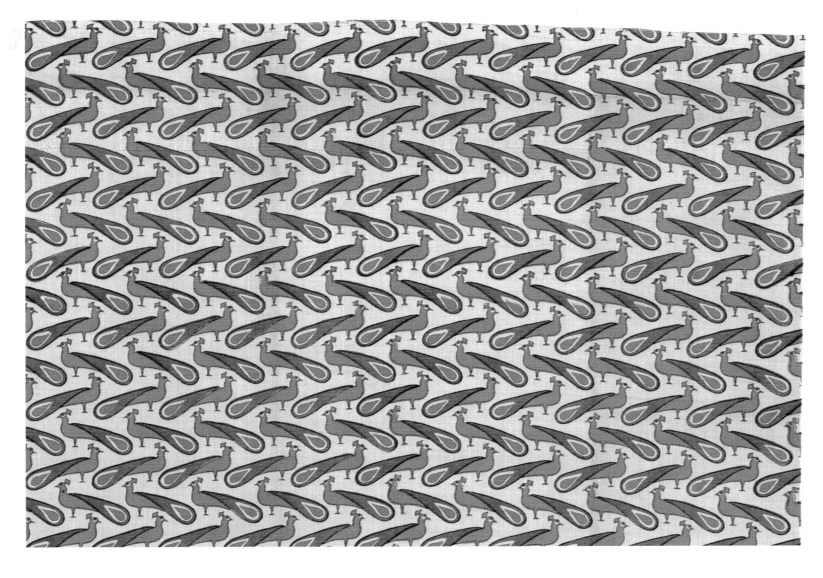

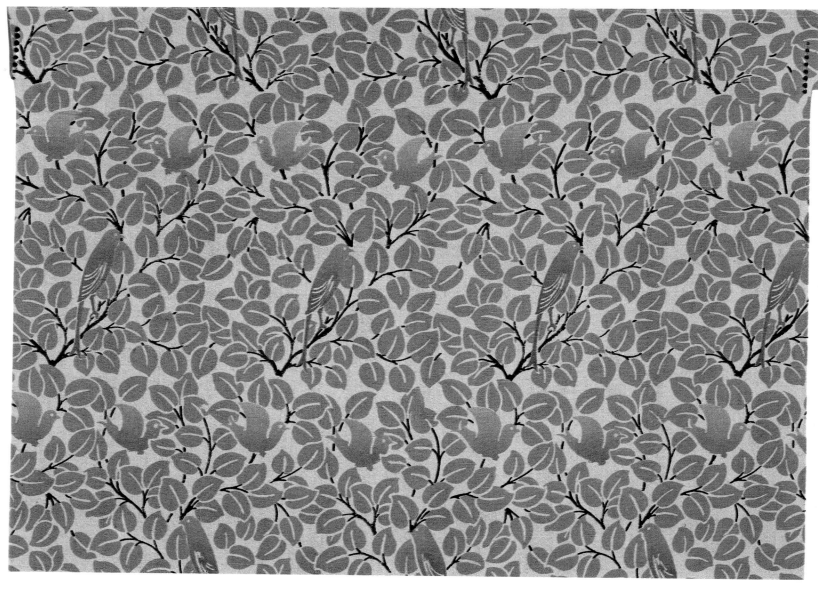

PLATE 53a

Roller-printed cotton manufactured by F. Steiner & Co. of Church in Lancashire in 1902. Possibly one of the many designs that this firm bought from the studio of Christopher Dresser.

PLATE 53b

Block-printed and indigo-discharged cotton. Designed by Sidney Mawson and printed by Thomas Wardle from about 1890. This design shows Mawson's early derivative style and has been mistaken for Morris's work.

PLATE 54a

Roller-printed cotton designed by Lindsay P. Butterfield. Manufactured from 1901 by Turnbull and Stockdale.

PLATE 54b

Roller-printed cotton. A Liberty Art Fabric *manufactured between 1896 and 1900 and sold in the shop for one and fourpence a yard.*

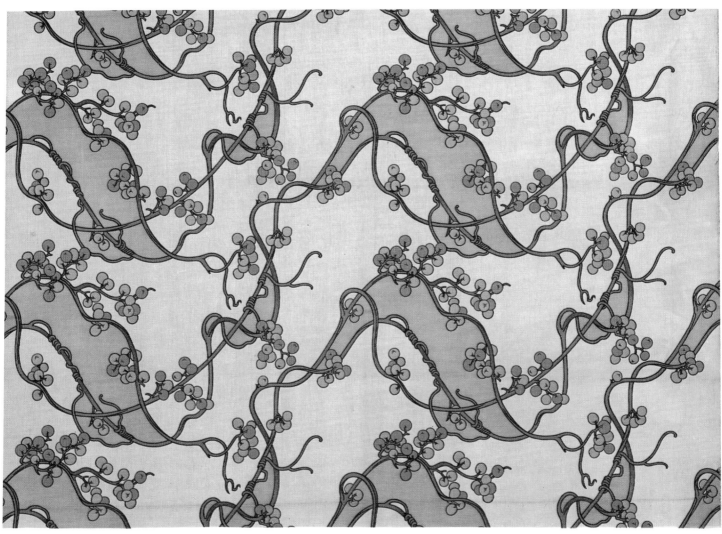

PLATE 55

Watercolour design for a stencil by Walter Crane. Probably drawn at the end of the 19th century when this type of decoration was at its most popular.

WALTER·CRANE

PLATE 56a

Watercolour design for a woven textile by C.F.A. Voysey c.1900. Bought from the designer by Alexander Morton & Co. No examples of cloth woven from this design are known.

PLATE 56b

Watercolour design for textile by C.F.A. Voysey, c.1897–9. Produced as a silk and wool double cloth by Alexander Morton & Co.

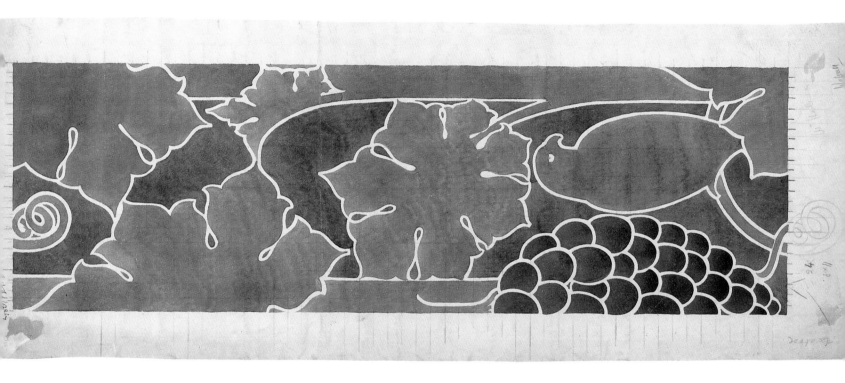

PLATE 57

Iris, *watercolour design for a textile by Walter Crane. Signed and dated 1903. An unusual example of a non-figurative design by Crane. It is unlikely that this design was put into production.*

IRIS.

Walter Crane 03

PLATE 58a

Union of Hearts, *a watercolour design for textile by C.F.A. Voysey, 1899.
The design was used by Alexander Morton & Co. as a woven fabric and as a
wallpaper by Essex & Co.*

PLATE 58b

*Watercolour design by Cecil Miller about 1904. The design was bought from
the artist by Alexander Morton & Co.*

PLATE 59

Rose and Acanthus *a pencil, ink and watercolour design by Sidney Mawson. Manufactured as a block-printed linen by G.P. & J. Baker about 1900.*

PLATE 60a

Holmwood, *pencil and watercolour design by Lindsay P. Butterfield, 1902. Produced by G.P. & J. Baker as a roller-printed cotton.*

PLATE 60b

Watercolour and pencil design by Lindsay P. Butterfield about 1905. Probably intended as a woven textile, the design was not put into production.

PLATE 61

Watercolour design for a textile by C.F.A. Voysey, 1901. Woven as a silk and wool double cloth by Alexander Morton & Co.

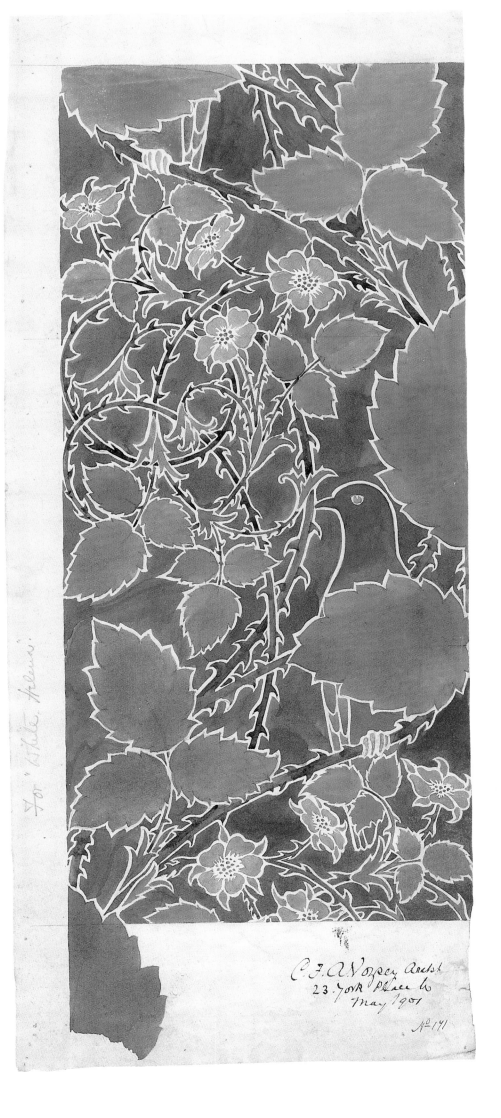

For "White Helene".

C.F.A. Voysey Artist
23. York Place W
May 1901

No 171

PLATE 62a

Border design for Japanese Rose *textile, watercolour on textured paper by George Rigby.*

PLATE 62b

Japanese Rose, *a watercolour design on textured paper by George Rigby. Together with its border it was block-printed as a bedcover by G.P. & J. Baker in 1903.*

PLATE 63

Watercolour design by G.R. Kennerley c.1896. Produced as a printed textile by G.P. & J. Baker for Liberty & Co. A matching border design also survives so it is likely that the two were used for bordered bedcovers which were very popular at this time.

PLATE 64a

Watercolour design by Harry Napper which was manufactured as a block-printed cotton by G.P. & J. Baker from 1909. Napper's work is often timeless and this design could well have been drawn ten years earlier.

PLATE 64b

Twyford, *a watercolour design by Lindsay P. Butterfield. Manufactured by G.P. & J. Baker in 1903 as a printed textile, and as a woven gauze a year later by Alexander Morton & Co.*

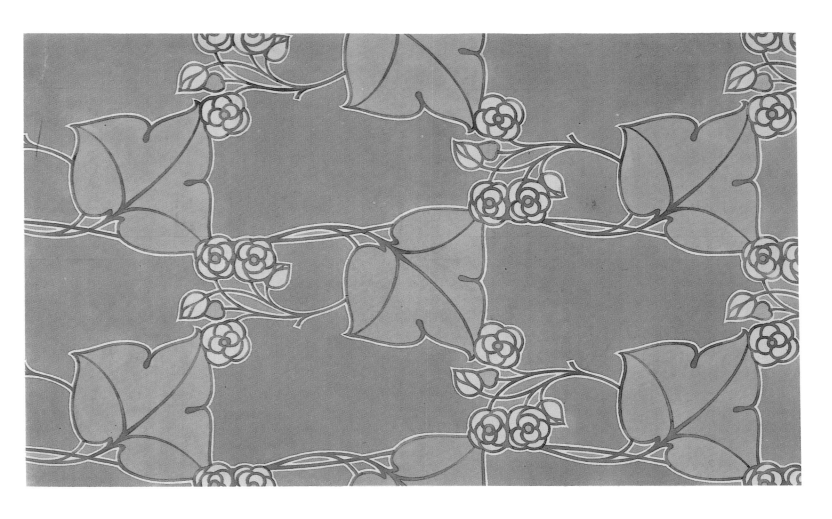

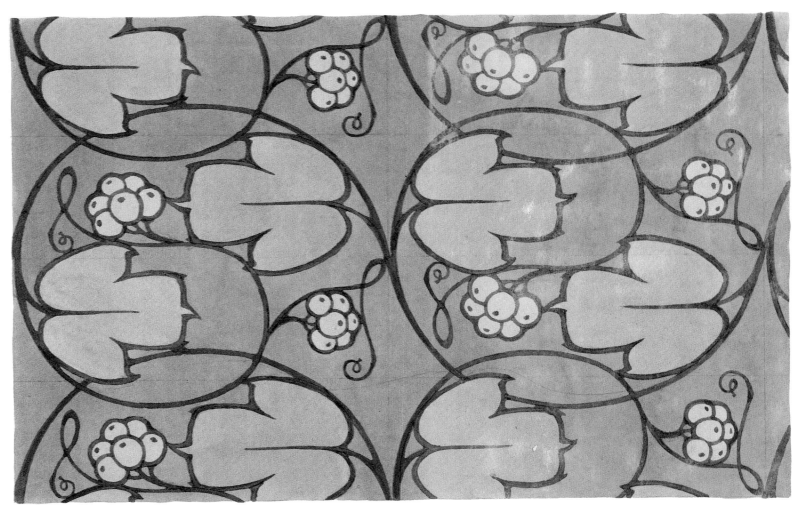

PLATE 65

Watercolour design for a textile. Manufactured as a block-printed fabric for Liberty & Co. at G.P. & J. Baker's Swaisland Print Works in Crayford between 1898 and 1899.

PLATE 66a

Canterbury Bell, *a watercolour design by Lindsay P. Butterfield.*
Manufactured as a roller-printed fabric by G.P. & J. Baker about 1902.

PLATE 66b

Caversham, *a watercolour design. Manufactured as a roller-printed cotton*
by G.P. & J. Baker from 1904. The designer is unrecorded but the eccentric
stylised motifs and sub-Voysey birds suggest the work of Harry Napper.

PLATE 67a

King Cup, *ink and watercolour design for a textile by Jessie Marion King about 1925. Printed by Thomas Wardle for Liberty & Co.*

PLATE 67b

Pencil and watercolour design for a textile. Drawn by Charles Rennie Mackintosh about 1918.

PLATE 68a

Gouache design for a printed textile. Produced by the Silver Studio in 1899. The Studio adopted many of the fashionable styles of the period and in this example shows their skill in producing carefully drawn flower patterns in the style of Lindsay P. Butterfield.

PLATE 68b

Watercolour design for a printed textile. Produced by the Silver Studio in 1903. This pattern illustrates the fashion for topiary and other forms of stylised garden trees in the early 20th century.

PLATE 69a

Vipers Grass, *roller-printed cotton gauze. Designed by Arthur Willcock, late 19th century. Little is known of this talented designer's work beyond the fact that he was very popular abroad and sold his patterns to many British and foreign manufacturers.*

PLATE 69b

Embroidered cushion cover. Designed and bought from Morris & Co. worked about 1896 by Miss Annie May Hegeman of New York.

PLATE 70

Machine-woven Wilton carpeting. Manufactured by the Bigelow Carpet Co. of Clinton, Massaschusetts, about 1909. One of the longest established American carpet factories. The pattern of both the field and border of this example is closely based on the work of British Arts and Crafts designers.

PLATE 71

Reversible woven cotton double-cloth manufactured by Alexander Morton & Co. The cloth was bought for the Trondheim collection from Hirschwald's Berlin shop, Hohenzoller Kaufhaus, in 1902 when it cost 6 marks a metre.

PLATE 72

*Woven silk and cotton double cloth. Manufactured by Alexander Morton &
Co. about 1898 and possibly designed by Lindsay P. Butterfield. The silk was
bought from Liberty & Co.*

PLATE 73

Crown Imperial block-printed silk. Designed by Lindsay P. Butterfield and printed by Thomas Wardle who registered the design on December 18th 1893. Now in Oslo, the design was bought in Berlin.

PLATE 74a

Block-printed velveteen probably manufactured by G.P. & J. Baker at their Swaisland print Works in Crayford about 1893. It is likely that the fabric was printed for Liberty & Co., whose use of peacock feather designs at this time had provided the shop with an unofficial trademark.

PLATE 74b

velveteen. Another design showing a variation of the Crown Imperial plant. A British fabric sold by Steen & Strøm, Christiania (now Oslo) in 1896.

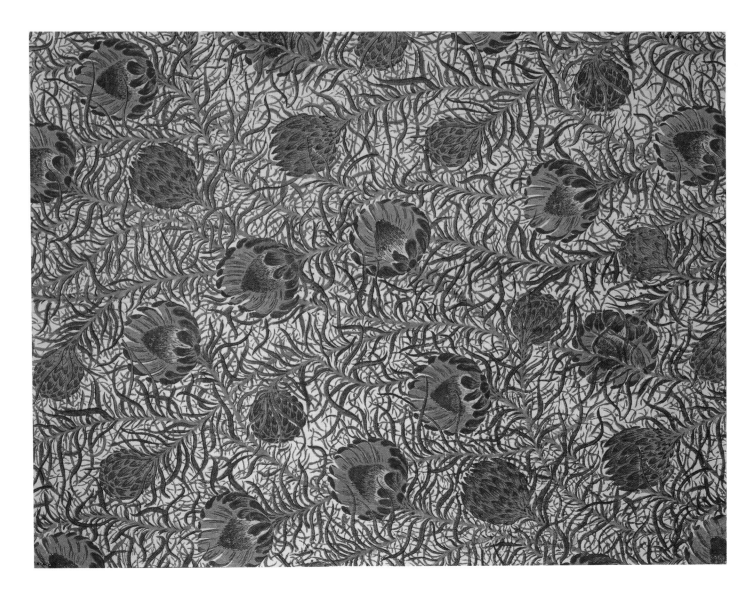

PLATE 75

Block-printed velveteen. The British design shows the use of a small subsidiary pattern much in the manner of William Morris although the tulips are much more haphazard and modernist in style. Bought in Berlin in 1894 for the Copenhagen Museum of Applied Arts.

PLATE 76a

Block-printed velveteen. The bird design is very similar to a pattern from "Atelier Willcock" now in Mulhouse, which may indicate that it was designed by Arthur Willcock. The cloth was manufactured about 1895.

PLATE 76b

Woven cotton fabric. A British design probably manufactured in northern France. Bought from Berlin in 1894.

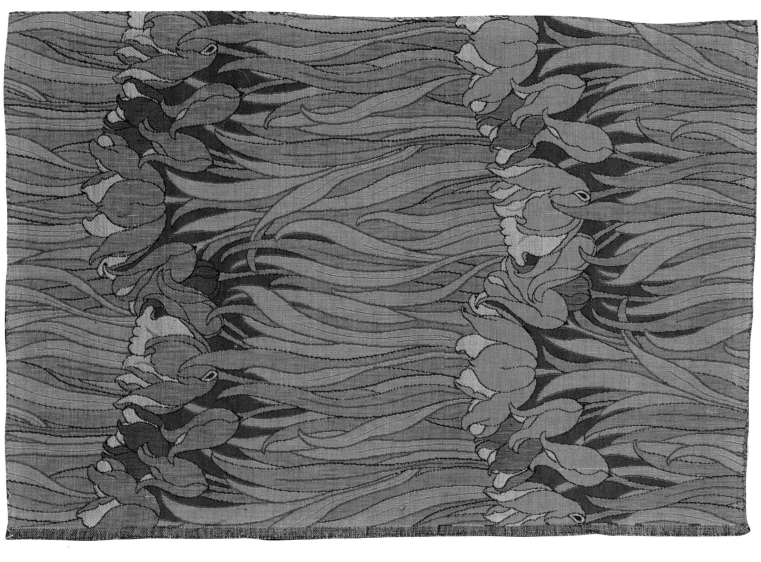

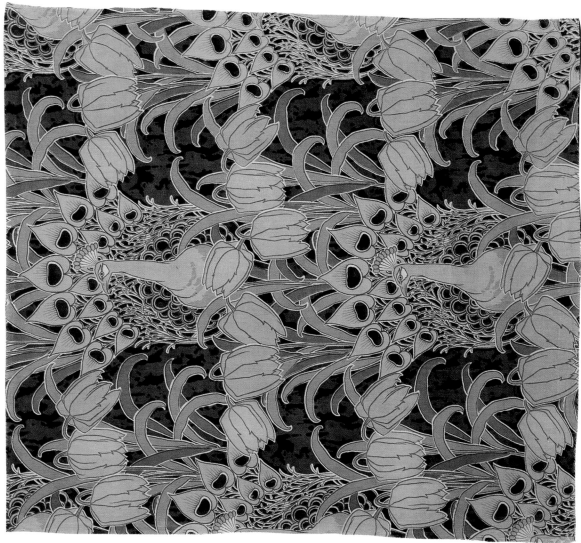

PLATE 77

Water Iris, *printed velveteen designed by Felix Aubert (1866–1943).
Manufactured by Pilon et Cie, Paris from 1897. Aubert was one of the most
influential Continental Art Nouveau designers. Although more formal in
repeat, this pattern shows a less stylised and more British use of floral
decoration than is usual in his work.*

PLATE 78a

Printed cotton designed by Walter Leistikow (1865–1908). Manufactured in Berlin about 1900. This tulip design is very similar to early Voysey textiles which were available from the mid 1890s in such shops as Hohenzoller Kaufhaus, Berlin.

PLATE 78b

Printed cotton manufactured by Louis Besselièvre Fils, Maromme, France, 1901. The pattern shows a strong influence of British patterns both in its colour and choice of subject.

PLATE 79

Printed cotton designed by Peter Behrens (1868–1940), between 1903 and 7. In common with British designers, Behrens, Germany's most important architect and decorative designer of the early 20th century, was keen to escape the unnatural curves of Art Nouveau. This design develops stylised bird forms in a similar way to Voysey's work but the result is quite different

PLATE 80

Woven silk designed by Georges de Feure (1868–1943). Woven in France by Marjorelle and bought from Bing's Maison de L'Art Nouveau *in 1906. One of the most stylish of Art Nouveau designers, de Feure's pattern shows the unmistakable influence of contemporary British patterns which were also available for sale in Bing's shop.*

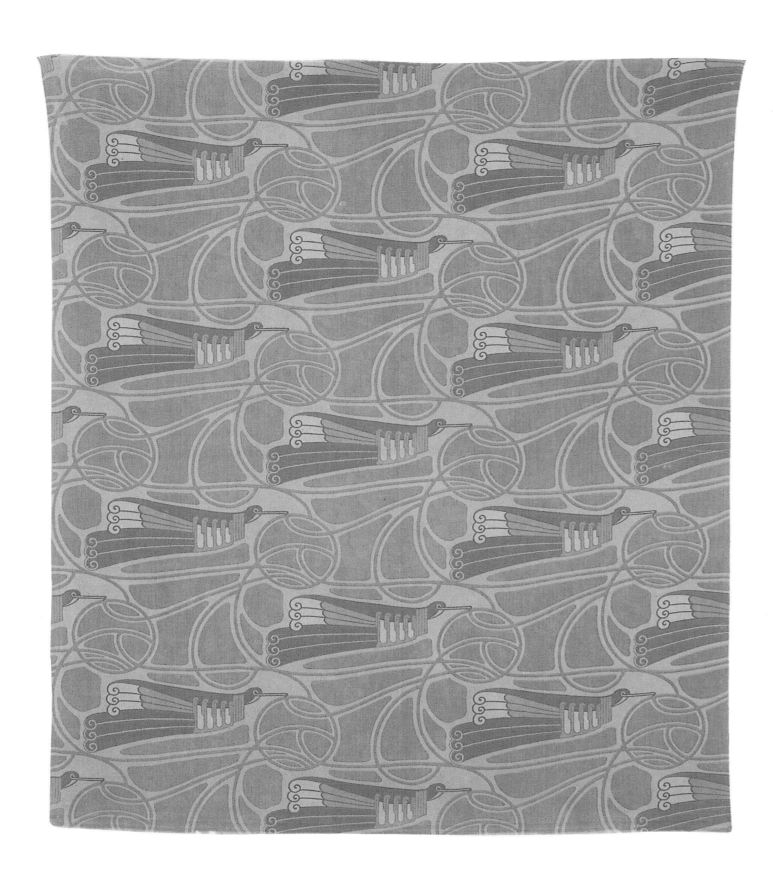

PLATE 81

Carpet designed by William Morris (1834–1986) England, early 1880s. Wool pile on cotton plain-weave foundation. Carpets, textiles and wallpapers designed by William Morris were used in the Glessner house in Chicago. This large carpet is particularly noteworthy.

PLATE 82

Cloth of Gold painted panel. Designed by Associated Artists, painted by Dora Keith c. 1895. Oil-based paint on silk warp metallic weft twill fabric. Allowing for the slight variation caused by hand painting rather than block printing, the design is the same as one by Associated Artists discharge-printed on blue cotton twill.

PLATE 83

Printed fabric with design of scallop shells and ribbons. Designed by Associated Artists New York, 1880s. Plain-weave cotton. Following the example previously set in England by the Century Guild, Associated Artists have incorporated their own initials, a double capital letter A, into the design. Fabric with this design was used as pillow covers in the Mark Twain home in Hartford, Connecticut

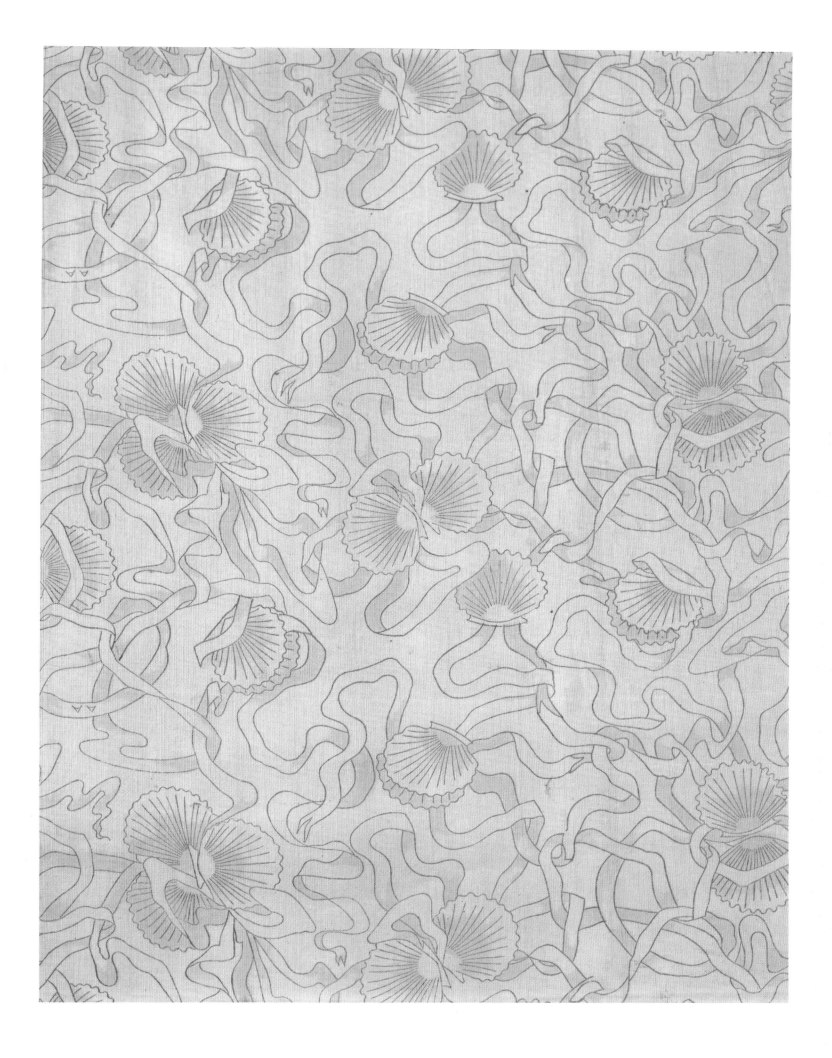

PLATE 84a

Printed fabric with design of nasturtium leaves. Designed by Associated Artists New York, 1880s. Plain-weave cotton. Seen here in blue on a natural ground, Associated Artists also produced this monochrome design in brown and maroon. The monogram, a double letter A, is upside down in relation to the nasturtium leaves on all of them.

PLATE 84b

Printed fabric with design of lilies and bubbles. Designed by Associated Artists New York, 1880s. Plain-weave cotton. There is a strong Japanese feeling to this fabric, which again includes the double letter A in the design. Associated Artists may have produced the printed fabrics themselves, in their workrooms in Fifth Avenue.

PLATE 85a

Pine cones *woven fabric. Designed by Associated Artists; produced by Cheney Bros. South Manchester, Connecticut; c. 1890. Silk. Associated Artists, under the guidance of Candace Wheeler, often used designs taken from native and familiar plants.*

PLATE 85b

Water Lily *warp-printed fabric. Designed by Associated Artists; produced by Cheney Bros. South Manchester, Connecticut; 1890s. Silk, twill weave. Warp-printed silks were described by Candace Wheeler as 'shadow silks' The design was printed on the warp yarns before the fabric was woven. In the weaving process the copper coloured weft yarns, interlacing with the printed warp, created the blurred edges of the pattern.*

PLATE 86

*Woven fabric with a design of thistle plants. Designed by Associated Artists;
produced by Cheney Bros. South Manchester, Connecticut; c. 1890. Silk,
twill damask. This design was also woven on a heavier weight fabric, strong
enough to be used as wall covering. The pattern, perhaps in both weights of
fabric, was used in Andrew Carnegie's summer home on the Berkshire
Mountains of Massachusetts, an obvious reference to Carnegie's Scottish
birth.*

PLATE 87

Panel with embroidery and appliqué. Designed and made by The Society of Blue and White Needlework, Deerfield, Massachusetts, about 1910. Foundation cloth, appliqué and embroidery threads are all of linen. Red embroidery on the red flower at the top reflects a sophisticated sense of colour. Using the same colour sensitivity, the signature D within a spinning wheel is in blue embroidery on a blue background in the lower left-hand corner.

PLATE 88

Seaweed and Dragonflies *embroidered table cover. Designed and made by The Society of Blue and White Needlework, Deerfield, Massachusetts, about 1915. Linen embroidery threads and foundation cloth. By 1915 the design had moved a long way from the blue and white embroidery of the early pieces. Table covers were probably the item the society produced more frequently than any other.*

PLATE 89

Embroidered doily. Designed and made by The Society of Blue and White Needlework, Deerfield, Massachusetts, about 1900. Linen embroidery threads and foundation cloth. Embroidery done in blue threads on a white cloth was the first work the society produced. Designs drew heavily on 18th century examples. The trademark of the society, a capital letter D within a spinning wheel, can be seen on this piece.

PLATE 90a

Syrian Olive Tree *batik panel. Designed and executed by Lydia Bush-Brown (1887–1984) New York; about 1923. Silk. Lydia Bush-Brown spent a year in Syria and when she returned to New York Syrian scenes appeared in her work. At the lower right of the field is the artist's distinctive monogram, her initials combined with a stylised beech tree and a circle to symbolise strength and insight.*

PLATE 90b

The Flowering Tree *batik panel. Designed and executed by Lydia Bush-Brown (1887–1984) New York, about 1922. Silk. The distinctive signature is at the right, just outside the walled city.* The Flowering Tree *is another batik from the Syrian series.*

PLATE 91a

Hunting *block printed panel. Designed and printed by George Biddle*
(1885–1952) New York, 1923. Silk, plain-weave.

PLATE 91b

Sailing *block printed panel. Designed and printed by George Biddle*
(1885–1952) New York, 1923. Silk, plain-weave. George Biddle, an artist
known for his paintings and lithographs, wrote of his work with block
printing on fabric and said it was the way a painter should begin his career.

PLATE 92

Woven curtains. Designed and woven at the Art School of H. Sophie Newcomb College, New Orleans, Louisiana; about 1920. Cotton; plainweave with supplementary wefts. Stylised trees and sailboats in the distance are on the curtain, probably woven under the direction of Gertrude Roberts Smith (1869–1962).

PLATE 93

Sailors Take Warning *tapestry woven panel. Designed and woven by Edith Huntington Snow (d. 1960) New York, about 1920. Silk and cotton. Edith Huntington Snow undertook private commissions and gave classes in weaving and other crafts.*

PLATE 94

Length of wallpaper. Produced by S.A. Maxwell Company Chicago, Illinois. Roller printed paper. When pasted on the wall, the vertical lengths of this unusual paper would create horizontal bands of pattern. The emphasis on green and the wood-grained background are responses to the visual criteria of the Arts and Crafts movement.

PLATE 95a

*Portières. Designed and made by Associated Artists, New York, 1890s.
Appliqué of pinwheel shapes in silk woven plush on a silk plain-weave
foundation. Portières, or curtains at the doorway, were an important part of
decorating schemes in the years around 1900. Here an interesting tonal
change is achieved as the colour of the appliqué shapes is very close to the
colour of the foundation cloth.*

PLATE 95b

*Woven rag rug. Used in Candace Wheeler's summer home in Onteora, New
York. Late 19th century. Cotton warp; silk and cotton woven fabric (rags)
weft. Woven rag rugs were discussed with admiration in Candace Wheeler's
writings. She wrote about tacking (sewing) the strips of woven fabric (rags)
together as the weaving progressed according to the desired colour.*

PLATE 96

Portières. Used in the Wheeler summer home in Onteora, New York. Designed and made by Associated Artists New York, 1890s. Embroidery on woven silk, border of brown silk velvet. Associated Artists frequently embellished the design on a woven or printed fabric with embroidery threads tracing the contours of the design. The combination of embroidery with other techniques was an early practice of Mrs. Wheeler's which was continued throughout her career.

PLATE 97

Consider the Lilies of the Field *embroidered and painted portières. Designed and made by Candace Wheeler, New York, 1879. Paint with stem and speckling stitches using wool on plain-weave cotton foundation. Mrs. Wheeler won first prize in 1879 at the Society of Decorative Arts when she entered this pair of portières in 1879. The text is complete only when both curtains are seen side by side. It became characteristic of Mrs. Wheeler's work to combine embroidery with another technique, in this case a painted cloth.*

PLATE 98a

Printed fabric. Designed and produced by Associated Artists New York, 1880s. Block-printed plain-weave cotton. Associated Artists used a creative approach to block printing in this fabric where the same block was printed with two different values of blue. Each block was vertically offset by 8 inches, creating a dimensional effect to the pattern.

PLATE 98b

Printed fabric. Designed and produced by Associated Artists, New York, 1890s. Block-printed and painted cotton velveteen. A printing block was cut for the ivy vine and printed in two different shades of blue, each impression slightly offset both vertically and horizontally. The yellow background was then hand painted onto the cloth.

PLATE 99

Printed fabric. Designed and produced by Associated Artists New York, 1890s. Block-printed plain-weave cotton. Five colours, each requiring its own set of printing blocks, were used to make the daylily design, making this one of Associated Artists more unusual and ambitious efforts.

PLATE 100

Portière. Design by George W. Maher (1864–1926) and Louis J. Millet (1853–1923) United States, 1901. Appliqué of cotton damask on cotton and silk velvet. Spiky thistles on the portière continue the design theme of the thistle which was used throughout the James A. Patten house in Evanston, Illinois.